START SMALL, THINK BIG

tiny, floating Coral

by Mary Auld

Consultants: Kirsten Golding of CoralWatch,
Dr Sally Keith and Dr Lisa Boström-Einarsson

illustrations by
La Scarlatte

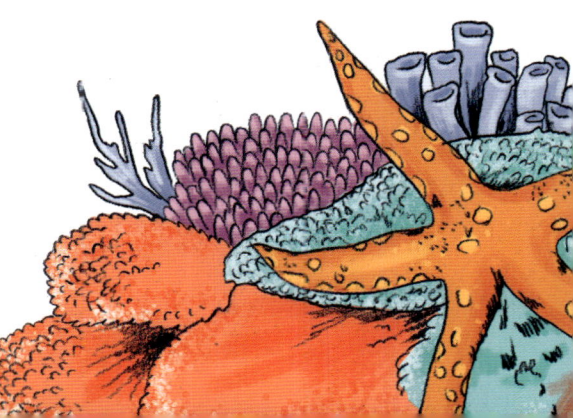

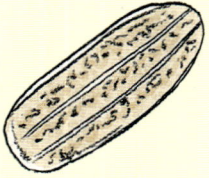

Here I am, a tiny floating coral planula. I am a minute animal drifting through the ocean, looking for the perfect place to live and grow.

A planula is the early stage in the life cycle of the tiny animals called polyps that form a coral reef.

Ocean water is full of microscopic life – lots of different plants and animals too small for us to see.

Here is a coral reef. I will settle here, where the sea is warm and calm. Can you find me?

Coral reefs grow in shallow water off the coast, in warm, tropical seas and oceans.

A planula usually settles on healthy coral reefs where there is lots of other life around.

A planula senses a good spot to grow. It uses tiny hairs to move down to a space on the reef.

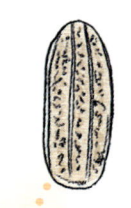

Here I am starting to settle. I am changing shape! My body becomes flat and I make a chalky substance to attach myself to the reef.

When it settles, a planula changes shape completely to become an adult polyp. This change is called metamorphosis.

Now I can reach out my tentacles into the water. They will collect things I need to grow and protect myself.

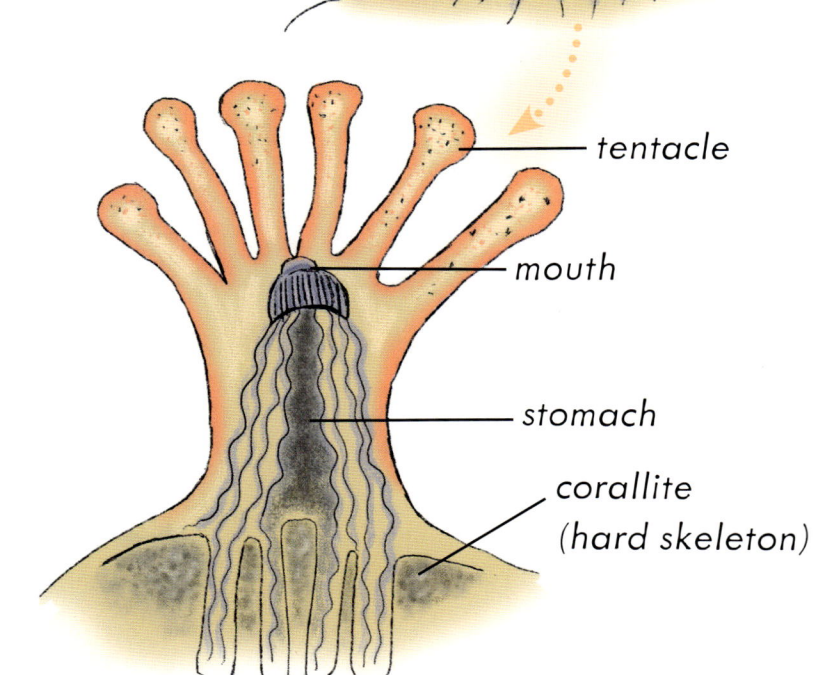

**Here I am splitting in two!
I am budding – making a new polyp.**
This new polyp will split, too. We do this
again and again. We will become a coral colony.

*A colony is group of animals
that lives and works together.*

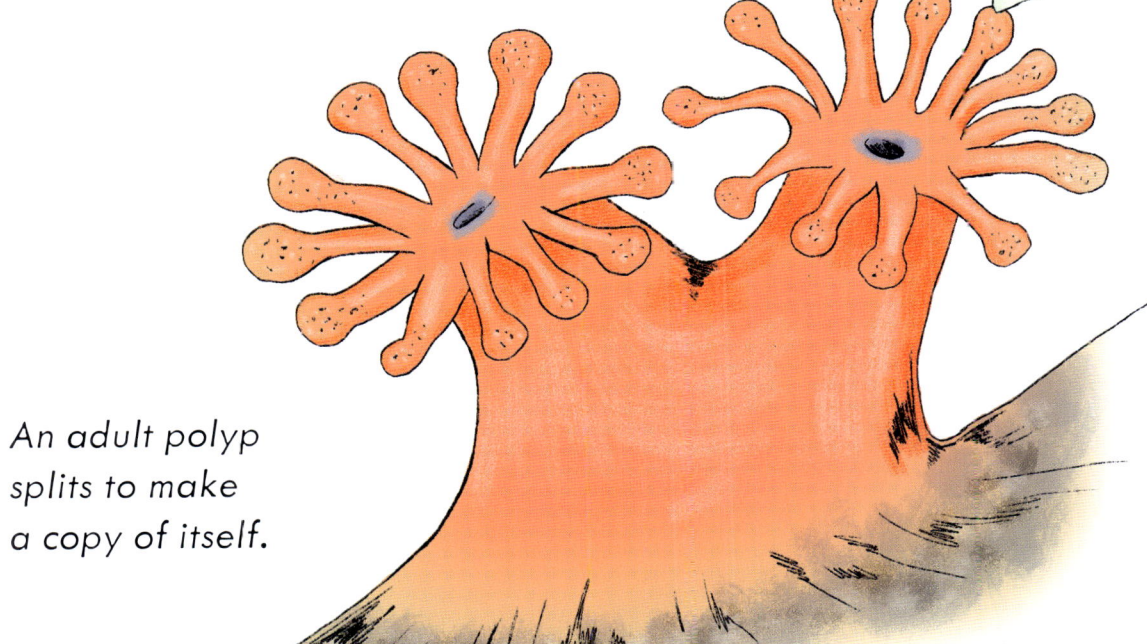

*An adult polyp
splits to make
a copy of itself.*

*Each polyp makes a hard skeleton,
connected to the previous one.
The hard skeletons build an
amazing shaped coral colony.*

Here is my colony. We are called smooth cauliflower coral. To grow fast, we need food!

Corals need energy to grow. They get some of this energy from microscopic food they catch in the seawater, but they need much more.

smooth cauliflower coral

We have a secret food supply. Tiny life forms called algae live inside us. Algae make food from sunshine and share their food with us.

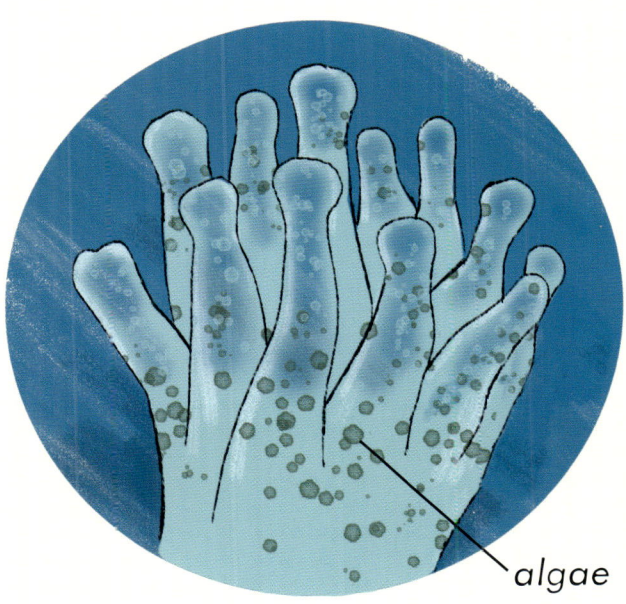
algae

The coral protects the algae inside its body. In return, the algae give some of their food to the coral.

The algae inside the coral polyps are called zooxanthellae (zoo-zan-thell-ay).

And look at the other coral growing around us.
We all have our own special shape and colour.

Hard corals build the reef, as the corallite under each polyp grows taller. Some form branching shapes.

plate coral
pillar coral
tube sponge
tube coral
branching coral

Soft corals, such as sea fans and whips, have more flexible bodies that move in the water.

sea fan

massive coral

purple whip fan

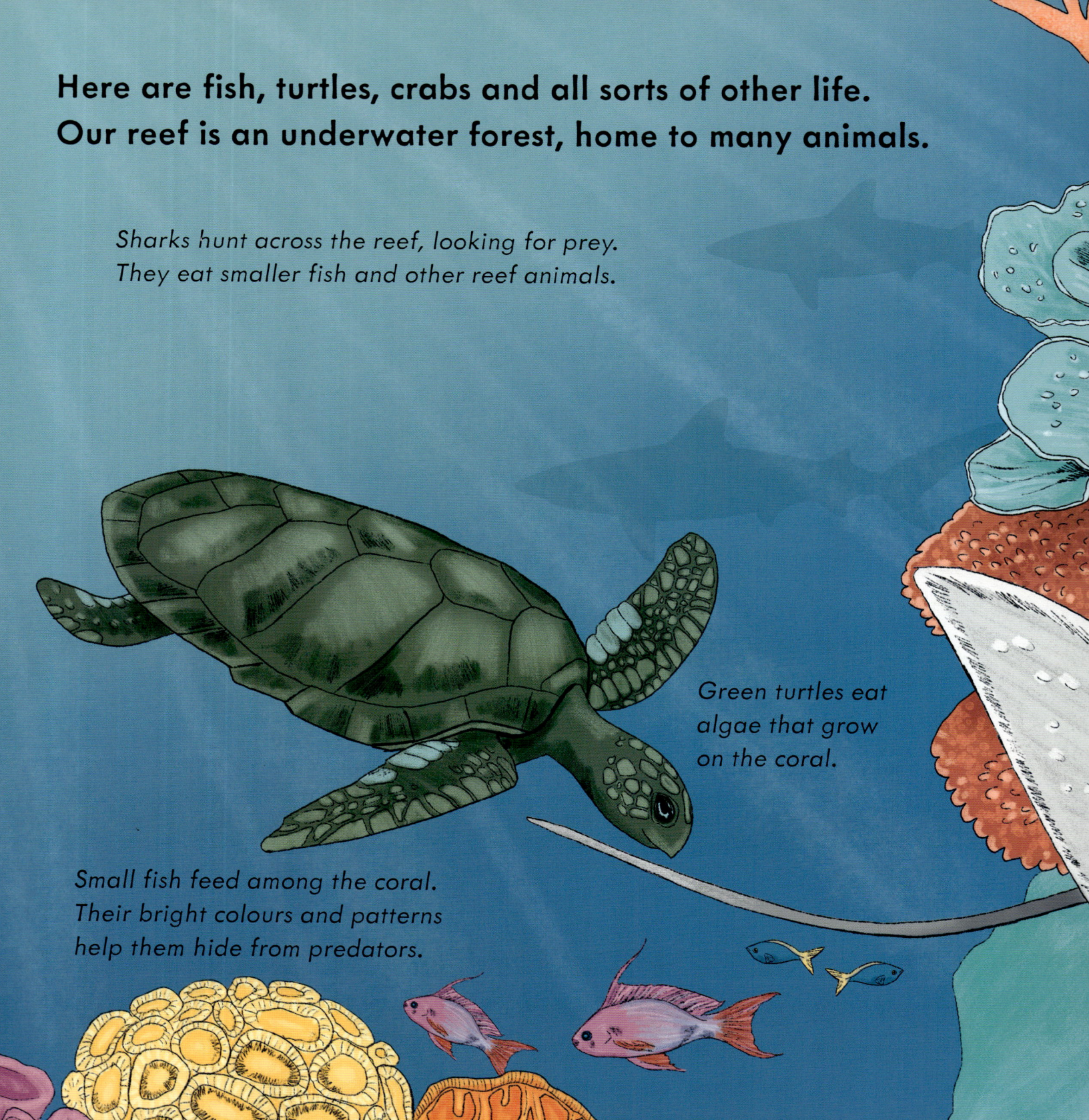

Here are fish, turtles, crabs and all sorts of other life. Our reef is an underwater forest, home to many animals.

Sharks hunt across the reef, looking for prey. They eat smaller fish and other reef animals.

Green turtles eat algae that grow on the coral.

Small fish feed among the coral. Their bright colours and patterns help them hide from predators.

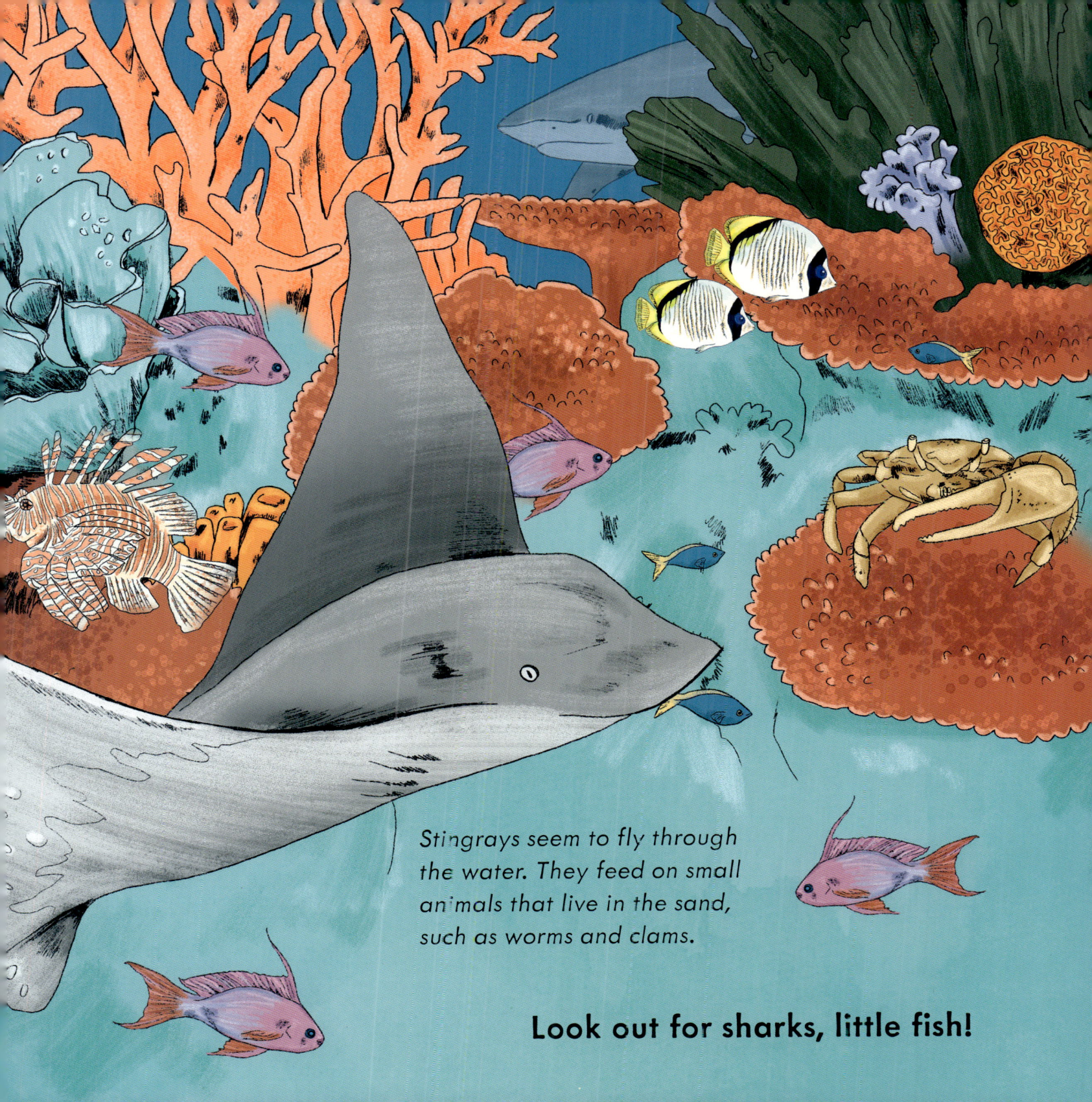

Stingrays seem to fly through the water. They feed on small animals that live in the sand, such as worms and clams.

Look out for sharks, little fish!

Here is our reef at night.
Night hunters look for prey hiding among us.

Small fish sleep hidden in the coral. This keeps them safe from predators, such as reef sharks.

Tiny shrimps hide in the coral by day but come out to feed at night.

Blackspotted puffer fish and lionfish are safe from predators because they are venomous.

At night, we all reach out our tentacles to catch food in the darkness.

Coral tentacles sting. They stun and catch their tiny prey, the microscopic life in the water. Those with long tentacles can pass food into their mouths.

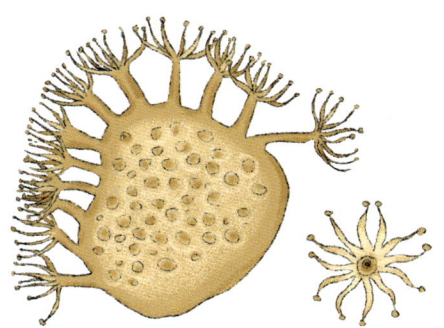

*Flowerpot coral
(Goniopora columna)*

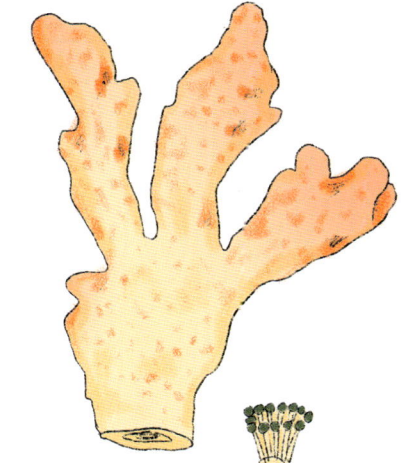

*Smooth cauliflower coral
(Stylophora pistillata)*

*Ivory bush coral
(Oculina varicosa)*

*Bird's nest coral
(Seriatopora hystrix)*

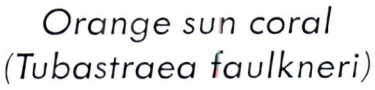

*Orange sun coral
(Tubastraea faulkneri)*

Here are islands formed by my reef. The reef lives and grows for thousands of years.

Reefs help to create beautiful beaches – safe places for baby turtles to hatch.

Pieces of dead coral and sand can pile up on part of a reef to form islands, called cays or keys. Birds bring seeds to the islands and plants begin to grow.

Here is the Great Barrier Reef, my reef's home. It is so huge it can be seen from space!

The Great Barrier Reef lies off the east coast of Queensland, Australia.

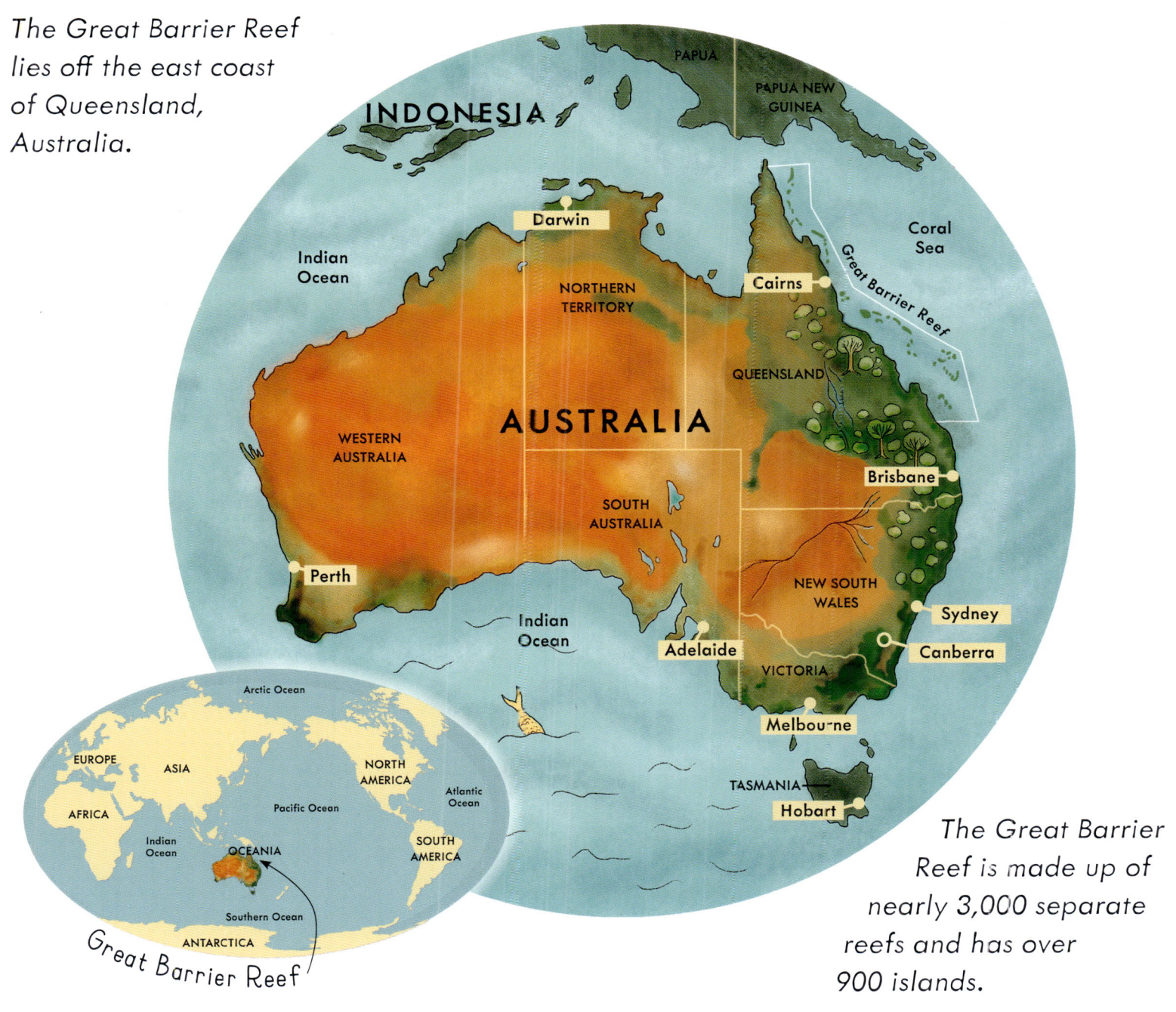

The Great Barrier Reef is made up of nearly 3,000 separate reefs and has over 900 islands.

Here is coral spawning. The moon is full and the tide is high. We are creating new life, spreading coral to other parts of the ocean.

Once a year, most hard corals give out tiny male and female gametes into the water. When they join together, they form a planula, a baby coral.

Fish, sea slugs and other sea creatures eat gametes, but the coral produce so many that enough survive.

We have made millions of new baby coral.
Most will be eaten but the rest will settle to form new colonies and new reefs.

Each newly formed planula floats with the ocean currents. It is part of the microscopic life, or plankton, that many sea animals feed on.

One of the largest plankton eaters is the whale shark. It sucks in water through its huge mouth and filters out its tiny food through its gills.